I0407919

Issued by Sandia National Laboratories, operated for the United States Department of Energy by Sandia Corporation.

SAND2012-2427
Unlimited Release
Printed March 2012

Cyber Threat Metrics

John Michalski, Cynthia Veitch
Critical Systems Security, 05621

Mark Mateski
Security Systems Analysis, 06612

Cassandra Trevino
Analytics and Cryptography, 05635

Jason Frye
Information Engineering, 09515

Mark Harris, Scott Maruoka
Assurance Tech and Assessments, 05627

Sandia National Laboratories
P.O. Box 5800
Albuquerque, New Mexico 87185-MS0671

Abstract

Threats are generally much easier to list than to describe, and much easier to describe than to measure. As a result, many organizations list threats. Fewer describe them in useful terms, and still fewer measure them in meaningful ways. This is particularly true in the dynamic and nebulous domain of *cyber* threats—a domain that tends to resist easy measurement and, in some cases, appears to defy *any* measurement.

We believe the problem is tractable. In this report we describe threat metrics and models for characterizing threats consistently and unambiguously.

This page intentionally blank

CONTENTS

FIGURES

TABLES

ACRONYMS AND ABBREVIATIONS

APT	Advanced Persistent Threat
C&C	Command and Control
CNO/CNE	Computer Network Operations and Exploitation
DHS	Department of Homeland Security
DOE	Department of Energy
FCEB	Federal Civilian Executive Branch
FNS	Federal Network Security
HSB	Human Studies Board
OTA	Operational Threat Assessment
RFP	Request for Proposal
RVA	Risk and Vulnerability Assessment
VAP	Vulnerability Assessment Program
VPN	Virtual Private Network
XSS	Cross-site Scripting

1 INTRODUCTION

For the purposes of this report, a *threat* is a person or organization that intends to cause harm. Threats are generally much easier to list than to describe, and much easier to describe than to measure. As a result, many organizations list threats, but fewer describe them in useful terms and still fewer measure them in meaningful ways.

Several advantages ensue from the ability to measure threats accurately and consistently. Good threat measurement, for example, can improve understanding and facilitate analysis. It can also reveal trends and anomalies, underscore the significance of specific vulnerabilities, and help associate threats with potential consequences. In short, good threat measurement supports good risk management.

Unfortunately, the practice of defining and applying good threat metrics remains immature. This is particularly true in the dynamic and nebulous domain of *cyber* threats—a domain that tends to resist easy measurement and, in some cases, appears to defy *any* measurement.

We believe the problem is tractable. In this report we describe threat metrics and models for characterizing threats consistently and unambiguously. We embed these metrics within a process and suggest ways in which the metrics and process can be applied and extended.

1.1 Background

The Department of Homeland Security (DHS) Federal Network Security (FNS) program created the Risk and Vulnerability Assessment (RVA) program to assist Federal Civilian Executive Branch (FCEB) agencies with conducting risk and vulnerability assessments [1]. These assessments individually identify agency-specific vulnerabilities and combine to provide a view of cyber risk and vulnerability across the entire federal enterprise. The RVA program has worked with Sandia National Laboratories to develop a basis Operational Threat Assessment (OTA) methodology that will result in an unclassified estimate of current threats to an FCEB system to be shared with the system owner [2].

The goal of the OTA phase of a risk and vulnerability assessment is to provide an accurate appraisal of the threat levels faced by a given FCEB agency. Information is collected about the system being assessed through document review and targeted searches of both open source and classified data sets. The identified threats, vulnerabilities, mitigations, and controls may be confirmed or discounted during assessment activities.

OTA is designed to provide an efficient threat estimate that is consistent from agency to agency and analyst to analyst. Given the scope of the RVA program, a large number of assessments will be conducted each year, addressing agencies with widely varying sizes and missions. The consistency and repeatability of each threat assessment is important to ensure similar treatment of all agencies and facilitate the combination of risk assessment results for all agencies. Toward this end, this report reviews cyber threat metrics and models that may potentially contribute to the OTA methodology.

1.2 Scope and Purpose

The purpose of this report is to support the OTA phase of risk and vulnerability assessment. To this end, we focus on the task of characterizing cyber threats using consistent threat metrics and models. In particular, we address threat metrics and models for describing malicious cyber threats to US FCEB agencies and systems.

1.3 Report Structure

This report is organized as follows:

- Chapter 1 provides background, scope, and purpose;

- Chapter 2 describes the nature and utility of threat metrics and models;

- Chapter 3 introduces the generic threat matrix and discusses its application as a threat model;

- Chapter 4 discusses several sources of possible threat metrics; and

- Chapter 5 concludes the report by sketching a threat analysis process.

2 THREAT METRICS AND MODELS

In order to define and apply good threat metrics, we must first understand the characteristics of a good metric and then understand how those metrics can be framed to establish a model to describe threat.

2.1 Threat Metrics

Before we discuss our approach to threat metrics, it is useful to review the following four questions.

What is a metric?
A concise dictionary definition of metric is "a standard of measurement" [3]. Similarly, a current security metrics guide describes a metric as "a consistent standard of measurement" [4]. Metrics allow us to measure attributes and behaviors of interest. A *meter*, for example, is a metric that allows us to measure length, while the *number of defects per shipment* is a metric that allows us to measure quality.

Confusion between a *metric* and a *measure* sometimes occurs. Bob Frost, a performance measurement authority, clarifies the terms by noting that "'metric' is the unit of measure, [while] 'measure' means a specific observation characterizing performance" [5]. Thus, if the number of defects per hour is the metric, the measure is the observed value of, for example, seven.

Why do we use metrics?
When we measure something using consistent metrics, we improve our ability to understand it, control it, and, in the case of a threat, better defend against it. According to the performance engineer H. James Harrington, "Measurement is the first step that leads to control and eventually improvement. If you can't measure something, you can't understand it. If you can't understand it, you can't control it. If you can't control it, you can't improve it." [6].

What makes a good metric?
A quality metric typically exhibits several conventional characteristics. For example, a good metric is clear and unambiguous. It facilitates inexpensive collection (that is, the cost of collecting measurement data doesn't exceed the value of the data). A good metric also supports decision making and precludes subjective interpretation.

Many authors further suggest that good metrics implement quantitative rather than qualitative scales. On this point, security professional Andrew Jaquith states that "good metrics should express results using numbers rather than high-low-medium ratings, grades, traffic lights, or other nonnumeric methods." He notes further that "Ordinal numbers— created by assigning a series of subjective scores numeric equivalents— are functionally equivalent to ratings" [4]. Although the goal of implementing only quantitative scales is certainly a worthy one, practitioners continue to debate precisely how to do this. For now, most organizations continue to implement qualitative scales for measuring "intangible" factors such as motivation and intent.

An additional factor to consider here is that no single metric—no matter how good it might be—is likely to tell the whole story. Multiple metrics from multiple perspectives are usually needed. This, in fact, is one of the driving ideas behind the widely used Balanced Scorecard that Bob Frost refers to as a "measurement framework" or a "performance model." Not only does a measurement framework help organize sets of metrics, Frost notes that it also "can tell you what types of variables to consider and where to look" [7].

What makes a good threat metric?

A good threat metric is foremost a good metric. It is clear and efficient, and it supports decision making. An example of a good threat metric might be number of attacks per month. If we are able to define attacks clearly and count them economically, we will most likely have a good metric. Over time, the count of attacks—whether high or low—grants the defender insight into the attacker's intent and capability. Given this, the defender can better calculate risk and allocate resources.

2.2 Threat Models

As we noted above, a stand-alone metric is usually insufficient to describe the characteristics or behavior of a complex system or actor. Much more useful is a "measurement framework" that combines metrics and their relationships into a complete and consistent whole. Although models can be much more than measurement frameworks, a measurement framework is certainly a model. In this section, we consider *threat models*. More specifically, we consider *cyber* threat models.

What is a threat?

We informally describe a threat as "a person or organization that intends to cause harm." More formally, a threat is "a malevolent actor, whether an organization or an individual, with a specific political, social, or personal goal and some level of capability and intention to oppose an established government, a private organization, or an accepted social norm" [8].

Threats can be of different types, and they can pursue different goals. Depending on the environment in which an information system or network is located and the type of information it is designed to support, different classes of threats will have an interest in attempting to gain different types of information or access, based on their particular capabilities.

What is a model?

Informally, a model is a simplified representation of something else. A model ignores, masks, or abstracts unimportant or unnecessary details, thereby highlighting the details of interest. For example, a model of a real-world computer network will abstract away certain details and highlight others.

What is a threat model? Clearly, a threat model is a model of a threat. Per the definition of *model* above, a threat model highlights the details of interest regarding a threat, class of threat, or threats in general. A threat model will generally address both a threat's capabilities and its intent.[1] Because our mandate is to address cyber threat metrics, the models we consider below emphasize the intent and capability of cyber threats.

Today, cyber threat models are frequently little more than a progression of semi-descriptive labels: *hackers*, *hacktivists*,[2] *script kiddies*,[3] *nation states*, *cyber terrorists*,[4] *organized crime*, or *malicious insiders*. These labels reinforce preconceived notions regarding motivation and resources. Unfortunately, this method undermines a clear understanding of capabilities—an understanding that is particularly useful when attempting to establish protections for an information system or network. The model that follows is designed to address the limitations of current cyber threat models.

Additionally, the model that follows is designed to promote consistency, even (or especially) when the analysis is performed by different analysts. Arming analysts with clearly defined, uniform threat models based on consistent metrics helps reduce the effects of personal bias and preconceived notions. Moreover, the value of consistency grows with time. Given a standardized threat model, an analyst can store consistent threat reports in a reference database accessible to other analysts. As new threats are encountered, these threats can be analyzed using the same process, allowing for up-to-date, accurate threat estimates that contribute to a consistent, repeatable, and reliable risk and vulnerability assessment process.

In the remainder of the report, we present and describe a threat model based on the generic threat matrix. We then discuss a range of possible metrics sources. We close by bringing these elements together into a broader threat assessment process.

---

[1] The *DHS Risk Lexicon* notes, for example, that "Adversary intent is one of two elements, along with adversary capability, that is commonly considered when estimating the likelihood of terrorist attacks ..." [11]

[2] A *hacktivist* uses computers and networks as a means of protest to promote social, political, or ideological ends.

[3] A *script kiddie* uses existing computer scripts or code to gain unauthorized access to data, but lacks the expertise to write custom tools.

[4] A *cyber terrorist* uses Internet-based attacks in terrorist activities, including acts of deliberate, large-scale disruption of computer networks.

This page intentionally blank

3   THE GENERIC THREAT MATRIX[5]

The generic threat matrix (Table 1) is currently used in the OTA methodology. Sandia developed the matrix in order to characterize and differentiate threats against targets of interest. The purpose of the matrix is to identify attributes that could help the analyst characterize threats based on their overall capabilities. This characterization allows for the description of the full spectrum of threat without assigning a label (with its preconceived notions) to a specific threat. Although it is impossible to capture each distinct type of threat consistently, the generic threat matrix enables government entities and intelligence organizations to categorize threat into a common vocabulary. Additionally, the generic threat matrix allows analysts in the unclassified environment to (1) identify potential attack paths that could be supported by the asserted capability and (2) identify proper mitigation steps to thwart attacks.

Table 1. Generic threat matrix

Threat Level	THREAT PROFILE						
	Commitment			Resources			
					Knowledge		
	Intensity	Stealth	Time	Technical personnel	Cyber	Kinetic	Access
1	H	H	Years to decades	Hundreds	H	H	H
2	H	H	Years to decades	Tens of tens	M	H	M
3	H	H	Months to years	Tens of tens	H	M	M
4	M	H	Weeks to months	Tens	H	M	M
5	H	M	Weeks to months	Tens	M	M	M
6	M	M	Weeks to months	Ones	M	M	L
7	M	M	Months to years	Tens	L	L	L
8	L	L	Days to weeks	Ones	L	L	L

Reproduced from Duggan et al. [8].

As presented in Table 1, the columns of the generic threat matrix describe possible attributes of a threat (described in further detail in the following sections), while the rows define the capability

---

[5] Portions of this section are reproduced from Duggan, D. P., Thomas, S. R., Veitch, C. K. K. and Woodard, L. *Categorizing Threat: Building and Using a Generic Threat Matrix*. Sandia Report SAND2007-5791, Sandia National Laboratories, Albuquerque, New Mexico, September 2007.

of a threat to act upon each attribute. A unique metric defines each attribute. Some of the metrics are quantitative (for example, the number of technical personnel), while others are qualitative (the level of cyber knowledge). From this perspective, the matrix is a framework or model for organizing a set of related metrics.

THREAT LEVEL 1 is the most capable of achieving an objective or goal, while LEVEL 8 is the least capable. In general, each threat level, from LEVEL 8 to LEVEL 1, represents a more dangerous threat than the previous level. Although a LEVEL 8 threat may be able to attain the same objective as a LEVEL 1 threat, it will be through an unprotected vulnerability of an asset, the fortuitous timing of an attack, or simple luck, rather than a capability characteristic possessed by the threat organization.

It is possible, indeed likely, that at least one specific threat—out of the full spectrum of threats—will not fit exactly into a specific threat level. In this case, the threat should be categorized into the level that has the most similar threat profile. This is the very reason that the generic threat matrix has been designed with levels-of-magnitude differences between subsequent threat levels: to ensure that a threat is not equally similar to two adjacent levels.

3.1 Threat Attributes

A threat attribute is a discrete characteristic or distinguishing property of a threat. The combined characteristics of a threat describe the threat's willingness and ability to pursue its goal. However, both willingness and ability are defined by multiple, separate attributes. The intent of this delineation of attributes is that each defines a distinctive characteristic of a threat and that no inherent dependencies exist between any two threat attributes.

There are two families of threat attributes: *commitment* attributes that describe the threat's willingness and *resource* attributes that describe the threat's ability.

3.1.1 Commitment Attribute Family

Commitment attributes are the characteristics of a threat that describe the threat's willingness to pursue its goal. Characteristics of commitment are indicative of a threat's capability because they exemplify the drive of the threat to accomplish its goal. Those threats with the highest commitment will stop at nothing in pursuit of the goal, while those with lower overall commitment will not display such drive and ambition.

There are three attributes in the commitment family:

- INTENSITY: The diligence or persevering determination of a threat in the pursuit of its goal. This attribute also includes the passion felt by the threat for its goal. Intensity is a measure of how far a threat is willing to go and what a threat is willing to risk to accomplish its goal. Threats with higher intensity are, therefore, considered more dangerous because of their driving ambition in pursuit of a goal.

- STEALTH: The ability of the threat to maintain a necessary level of secrecy throughout the pursuit of its goal. The maintenance of secrecy may require the ability to obscure any or all details about the threat organization, including its goal, its structure, or its internal

14

operations. A higher level of stealth allows a threat to hide its intended activities, as well as its internal structure, from the outside world. This hinders intelligence gathering and pre-emptive measures to counter, or prevent, attacks by the threat.

- TIME: The period of time that a threat is capable of dedicating to planning, developing, and deploying methods to reach an objective. In the case of a cyber or kinetic attack, it includes any time necessary for all steps of implementation up to actual execution. The more time a threat is willing and able to commit to preparing an attack, the more potential the threat has for devastating impacts.

Additional details regarding the levels of each attribute can be found in Duggan et al. [8].

3.1.2 Resource Attribute Family

Resource attributes are the characteristics of a threat that describe the people, knowledge, and access available to a threat for pursuing its goal. Characteristics of resources are indicative of a threat's capability because greater resources may allow a threat to accomplish an objective or goal more easily and with greater overall adaptability.

There are three attributes in the resource family:

- TECHNICAL PERSONNEL: The number of group members that a threat is capable of dedicating to the building and deployment of the technical capability in pursuit of its goal.[6] Technical personnel includes only group members with specific types of knowledge or skills, such as kinetic or cyber, and those directly involved with the actual fabrication of the group's weapons. A threat with a higher level of technical personnel has greater potential for innovative design and development, allowing for the possibility of new methods of reaching a goal that may not have been available in the past. In addition, a higher level of technical personnel also expedites the design and development of a threat's plans for attack.

- KNOWLEDGE: The threat's level of theoretical and practical proficiency and the threat's capability of employing that proficiency in pursuit of its goal. Knowledge also includes the ability of a threat to share information, acquire training in a necessary discipline, and maintain a research and development program. However, this attribute does not include any proficiency found or purchased outside the threat organization. This attribute includes knowledge pertaining to both an offensive and defensive capability within the category. The greater the knowledge of a threat as a whole, the more capability a threat has to pursue its goal with fewer resources and in less time. Also, a threat's knowledge provides a means to differentiate between threats that are cyber, kinetic, or hybrid-based. There are two basic categories of knowledge:

---

[6] The designation given to each level of TECHNICAL PERSONNEL (e.g., ONES or HUNDREDS) is intended as a relative measure only and does not necessarily limit or enumerate the actual physical count of active members in a threat organization. For example, a malevolent organization with a thousand members may have only fifty technical personnel capable of building and deploying weapons. Depending on the structure of the organization, the threat would have A TECHNICAL PERSONNEL capability of only TENS or TENS OF TENS.

- CYBER KNOWLEDGE: The theoretical and practical proficiency relating to computers, information networks, or automated systems.

- KINETIC KNOWLEDGE: The theoretical and practical proficiency relating to physical systems, the motion of physical bodies, and the forces associated with that movement.

- ACCESS: The threat's ability to place a group member within a restricted system—whether through cyber or kinetic means—in pursuit of the threat's goal. A restricted system is considered to be any system, whether cyber or physical, where access is granted based on privileges or credentials. The characteristic of access details a threat's ability to infiltrate a restricted system, whether through a privileged group member, the blackmail and coercion of an innocent bystander, or the corruption of an under-protected network or computer system. Infiltration by a threat can lead to a wide variety of effects: the need for fewer resources to achieve an objective, the implementation of a long-term scheme of product-tampering, or an increased level of intimate knowledge of a target.

Additional details regarding the levels of each attribute can be found in Duggan et al. [8].

3.2 Profiles of Threat Capability

There are several observations that can be made after review of the generic threat matrix. First, there are two boundary conditions necessary for establishing viable threat profiles:

- Threats with a LEVEL 1 profile will always have the highest capability within each attribute.

- Threats with the highest numbered level (LEVEL 8 in this matrix) will always have the lowest capability within each attribute.

Second, a threat's level of TECHNICAL PERSONNEL can aid in understanding a threat's other attributes:

- Threats with more TECHNICAL PERSONNEL will necessarily have greater INTENSITY, KNOWLEDGE, and ACCESS. This is based on the assumption that more personnel create more viable opportunities.

- Threats with a TECHNICAL PERSONNEL level of ONES will not have high KNOWLEDGE, because these threats have little capacity for information sharing or research and development programs.

- Threats with TECHNICAL PERSONNEL level of ONES will not have high INTENSITY because these threats are not likely to be self-sacrificing.

The level of KNOWLEDGE possessed by a threat organization also follows an observable pattern:

- Threats with high CYBER KNOWLEDGE will not have low KINETIC KNOWLEDGE—and vice-versa—because of the application of expert proficiency in both theoretical and practical domains.

A final observation can be made regarding a threat organization's capability for ACCESS:

- Threats with high KNOWLEDGE—CYBER or KINETIC—will have at least medium ACCESS due to the assumption that it is easier to attain and harder to detect access achieved through expert proficiency.

3.3 MITRE's Cyber Prep Methodology

The MITRE Corporation's Cyber Prep methodology [9] characterizes threats using an approach similar in many ways to the generic threat matrix [1].This is not surprising; the MITRE work cites two papers on the generic threat matrix papers as sources. The MITRE approach, for example, also defines *threat* as *the adversary*, and it characterizes threats using qualitative levels, in this case five: advanced, significant, moderate, limited, and unsophisticated.

The approach, however, differs in one major feature: It divides the threat attributes into three classes (capability, intent, and targeting)[7] rather than two (commitment and resources). It does not decompose the three classes, but it does describe example threats in which the values of the three classes vary more than they do in the generic threat matrix levels. For example, the paper cited above describes adversaries of low capability and intent and moderate targeting, and adversaries of high capability and low intent and targeting. The eight levels shown in Table 1 do not include these sorts of high-low mixes.

The generic threat matrix and the tabular threat characterization approach used in Cyber Prep are clearly cousins. Each has apparent strengths and weaknesses. The generic threat matrix offers the analyst a discrete set of adversary levels to consider. More can be generated, certainly, but the limited number will in many cases be an advantage. The analyst is not required to search a large space but instead looks for the closest approximation—a much easier task that is likely to be adequate in most cases. The generic threat matrix also includes both qualitative (STEALTH, KNOWLEDGE) and quantitative (TIME, TECHNICAL PERSONNEL) metrics, while Cyber Prep's metrics are strictly qualitative.

The Cyber Prep approach, on the other hand, does allow for differences in targeting. This can be useful, for example, when attempting to differentiate between (1) the adversary with low capability and intent but aggressive targeting and (2) the adversary with high capability, moderate intent, and low targeting. Advocates of the generic threat matrix can argue that "intent" addresses both capability and intent and that the two are correlated. Still, the Cyber Prep approach clearly allows for more granular descriptions of adversaries, at least at the level of capability, intent, and targeting.

---

[7] *Targeting* is defined by MITRE as "how broadly or narrowly and how persistently the adversary targets a specific organization, mission, program, or enterprise."

This page intentionally blank

4 ADDITIONAL SOURCES OF THREAT METRICS

The generic threat matrix is a useful threat model. It does not, however, capture all possible threat metrics. The following sections outline some additional sources of threat metrics. Some of these supplement and enhance the generic threat matrix, while others offer an independent perspective.

4.1 Incident Data

In this section, we describe some of the categories of incident information that may be used to assess and measure the attributes of a threat.

The variables of interest in a complex system may or may not be directly observable. For instance, a network-based cyber-attack on an information system is directly observable if the network data are collected, but the particular size and composition of the threat is not necessarily observable through the same means. The magnitude of a threat's attributes must often be estimated using some indirect method, such as statistical data analysis, expert opinion, or intelligence analysis. In Table 2, we present some example categories of information that may be gleaned from incident reports in order to contribute to the analysis of a threat's capabilities. Note in particular the final column, which specifies the expected relation of the information category to the threat attributes in the generic threat matrix.

Table 2. The expected relationship between incident details and threat attributes.

Category	Incident Details Related to Classification	Expected Relation to Threat Attributes

Incident Characteristics	• What type of incident occurred (e.g., website defacement, denial of service, unauthorized access, reconnaissance/probing)?
	
	• If malicious software (e.g., a virus or Trojan) was involved in the incident, was its purpose
	    • Command and control (C&C)?
	    • Remote access?
	    • Data exfiltration?
	    • Data manipulation?
	    • Activity monitoring?
		TECHNICAL PERSONNEL
		
		CYBER KNOWLEDGE

Target System Characteristics	• Was the level of security protection on the target system
	    • High—fully protected using access control, file monitoring, up-to-date patches, etc.?
	    • Moderate—some protections implemented?
	    • Low—very limited protections implemented?
		TECHNICAL PERSONNEL
		
		CYBER KNOWLEDGE
		
		ACCESS

Timeline	• What is the date of initial activity related to incident? • What is the most recent date of activity related to incident? • On what date was the incident detected?	INTENSITY STEALTH TIME

Category	Incident Details Related to Classification	Expected Relation to Threat Attributes

Covert Activity	• Was activity related to the incident identified by
	  • Network monitoring?
	  • A monitoring application (e.g., intrusion detection system or anti-virus software)?
	  • A system administrator?
	  • A system user?
	• Were identified activities immediately associated with the incident? Or were identified activities originally dismissed as false alarms?
	• Were event logs or timestamps modified or deleted to obfuscate activity associated with the incident?
	• Were file/disk deletion tools involved in the incident?
	• Were incident activities related to reconnaissance, probing, execution, or exploitation stages of attack?
		STEALTH
		CYBER KNOWLEDGE
		ACCESS

Attack Vector	• Was the incident facilitated by
	  • Phishing?
	  • Social engineering (other than phishing)?
	  • Remote access (e.g., VPN or modem)?
	  • Inside access?
	• If the attack was facilitated by any type of social engineering, including phishing, was it a targeted, individual approach or a broad blanketing approach?
		STEALTH
		TIME
		CYBER KNOWLEDGE
		ACCESS

Attack Sophistication	• Was more than one computer system affected by this incident? • Was the internal network accessed on multiple occasions during this incident? • Were activities associated with the incident novel in any way (i.e., a zero-day attack) or common (i.e., easily acquired toolsets)?	STEALTH TIME CYBER KNOWLEDGE ACCESS
Anti-virus Signature	• Does an anti-virus signature (from any vendor) exist for any malicious software involved in the incident? • If so, did the signature exist and was it widely available on the date of initial activity?	TECHNICAL PERSONNEL CYBER KNOWLEDGE
Physical Interaction	• Was the system physically accessed as part of the incident? • Was the incident facilitated via the introduction of a physical medium (e.g., USB drive, CD, hardware)? • Did the incident result in any physical, real-world effects?	TECHNICAL PERSONNEL KINETIC KNOWLEDGE ACCESS
Obfuscation	• Was any involved malicious software encrypted or packed? • Was any activity, function, or script injected into another for malicious purposes?	STEALTH TECHNICAL PERSONNEL CYBER KNOWLEDGE

Category	Incident Details Related to Classification	Expected Relation to Threat Attributes

Data Compromise	• Was data compromised (e.g., manipulated, exposed, deleted) in relation to the incident? If so,
	  • What type of data (e.g., OUO, PII, SUI, UCNI) was compromised?
	  • Did compromised data affect system operation or mission?
	• Was data exfiltrated as part of the incident? If so,
	  • What type of data (e.g., password hashes, PII, OUO, UCI, proprietary, military, security) was exfiltrated?
	  • Was data exfiltrated on multiple occasions?
	  • Was data encrypted as part of the exfiltration process?
		INTENSITY
		STEALTH
		TIME
		CYBER KNOWLEDGE
		ACCESS

Attribution	• Is it possible to definitively attribute the activities associated with the incident to a specific actor?
	• Has any group or individual claimed responsibility for the incident?
	  • If so, was the statement public or private? Was the statement a general, specific, or limited declaration?
	  • Has any group or individual made a targeted threat statement against the victim organization?
	• Were hop-points used? If so, how many?
	• Did the attack originate from a U.S. or foreign IP address? If the source IP address is in another country, which country?
		INTENSITY
		STEALTH
		TECHNICAL PERSONNEL
		CYBER KNOWLEDGE

Table 3 summarizes the relationships contained in Table 2.

Table 3. The relationship between incident information categories and threat attributes.

Criteria	Attribute						
	Commitment			Resources			
					Knowledge		
	Intensity	Stealth	Time	Technical personnel	Cyber	Kinetic	Access
Incident				✓	✓		
Target system				✓	✓		✓
Timeline	✓	✓	✓				
Covert activity		✓			✓		✓
Attack vector		✓	✓		✓		✓
Sophistication		✓	✓		✓		✓
AV Signature				✓	✓		
Physical interaction				✓		✓	✓
Obfuscation		✓		✓	✓		
Data compromise	✓	✓	✓		✓		✓
Attribution	✓	✓		✓	✓		

4.2 Threat Multipliers

Additional properties of threat exist that, while not distinctive characteristics, can affect one or more threat attributes; they can enhance a threat's capabilities, but they do not affect the threat's profile level. Consider the following three multipliers, each of which can be quantified.

- FUNDING: The monetary support available to a threat has historically been used to define the capability of threat groups; however, because the value of currency fluctuates over time, it is a difficult factor to translate into actual capability. As a multiplier, FUNDING can be used to enhance certain threat attributes, such as KNOWLEDGE or ACCESS. On the other hand, it can also reduce the level of a threat attribute such as STEALTH—the purchase of greater KNOWLEDGE or increased access may make an organization more detectable because it is using outside resources.

- ASSETS: A threat's ability to have, build, or acquire the equipment, tools, and material necessary for the pursuit of its goal can be a difficult factor to translate into actual capability. However, like funding, it can enhance a threat's ability to carry out its mission.

- TECHNOLOGY: The type of technology that a threat is capable of utilizing or targeting in pursuit of its goal can be a limiting factor on certain threat attributes, such as TIME and KNOWLEDGE. The fast-paced, dynamic nature of some technology and its development requires up-to-date KNOWLEDGE and quick implementation or application.

4.3 Attack Vectors

An attack vector is an avenue or tool that a threat uses in order to gain access to a device, system, or network in order to launch attacks, gather information, or deliver/leave a malicious item or items in those devices, systems, or networks. An analyst can associate specific attack vectors with specific threat levels in the generic threat matrix (that is, certain vectors may require more commitment and resources, limiting them to the more sophisticated threat levels). An analyst, for example, might associate a given attack vector with THREAT LEVEL 2 through THREAT LEVEL 8 while another vector might be associated with THREAT LEVEL 1 through THREAT LEVEL 3. When performing this sort of assessment, the analyst extends the basic threat model contained in the generic threat matrix. Further work is needed to integrate the model fully, but it should be clear from the description of these vectors below and the content of Table 2 and Table 3 that attack vectors represent a potentially rich source of threat metrics.

In addition, each vector suggests a range of associated attack metrics. For instance, how much time does each vector take to plan, stage, and execute? How frequently does each level of threat execute each type of vector? Which vectors do attackers apply against which sorts of targets and vulnerabilities? Each of these questions corresponds to one or more metrics that the analyst can apply within the generic threat matrix or another threat model.

Not surprisingly, the number and sophistication of attack vectors grows as technology advances. The popularity of mobile computing offers threats more avenues and tools that they can use to launch attacks, gather information, or deliver/leave malicious applications. Some general attack vectors include the following.

- *Phishing attacks* can use a network's applications against its own users. For example, a company-wide email may include maliciously crafted links to viruses or malware. Additionally, detailed information regarding a network's users can be gathered on the Internet via public archives and social networking sites. This information can be used to conduct targeted phishing attacks against individual users that can be very difficult to detect.

- *Unsecured wireless networks* can be used as both a tool and an avenue for launching certain attacks. If attackers are able to gain unauthorized access to a wireless network, they can observe traffic, exfiltrated data, and deny services to legitimate users.

- *Removable media*, such as USB drives, can easily introduce malware into an information system. The threat doesn't need to be actively involved if an unsuspecting individual connects a USB drive of unknown origin to his own or his organization's computer system.

- *Mobile devices (e.g., smartphones and tablets)* can be used both as a tool and an avenue for launching attacks or gathering personal information. One example is when a threat makes use of the location where mobile users purchase "apps" for their smartphones. If a threat actor is able to create rogue apps or modify existing apps and an unsuspecting individual downloads such apps to her smartphone, the individual has opened up her mobile device to the threat. Mobile devices introduce potential vulnerabilities associated with physical loss and inconsistent configuration management (e.g., personally owned devices vs. enterprise owned).

- *Malicious web components* can be used as a tool for a threat to be able to launch attacks by possibly using malicious web pages. If an unsuspecting individual visits a malicious web page, he can possibly make his systems or networks vulnerable. Malicious downloads may occur as a result of visiting web pages that contain malicious web components (downloads). Insufficiently secured web components offer attack surfaces susceptible to SQL injection and cross-site scripting (XSS) attacks.

- *Viruses and malware* are tools that are used in order to launch certain types of attacks. Many of these tools are openly available on the Internet. Such attacks will have differing goals—based on the threat actor, environment, and target system/network.

The attack vectors listed above (and others not listed) can be used in conjunction to launch particular types of attacks. As threat actors become more sophisticated and attack methods become more portable, the list of attack vectors will continue to grow. Usually, attack or threat vectors are included in attack graphs or trees (see Section 4.5) to show where along an attack path they play a role.

4.4 Target Characteristics

Target characteristics also offer the analyst a source of metrics to relate to the threat model. These characteristics, for example, suggest that some targets are more attractive than others, that some targets are more vulnerable than others, and that some targets are targeted more frequently than others. If the analyst uses the generic threat matrix as his primary threat model, then information about target characteristics can inform the threat levels and can, in addition, be aggregated and associated with the threat levels as shown in Section 0.

Some characteristics of the target system can help an analyst to understand the existence or likelihood of threat action against that system. The following system characteristics are representative.

- The quantity or frequency of *unattributed cyber-attack incidents*, such as network probes, malware discoveries, Web-based attacks, phishing emails, spear phishing incidents, and exfiltrated data.

- The *availability of agency information* discoverable through publicly accessible means:

    - The quantity or percentage of agency personnel found on social sites and the amount of sensitive information posted by those personnel.

    - The inclusion of requests for proposal (RFPs), statements of work, design documentation, and configuration guidelines posted on public websites or available in open archives.

- The *value of the agency*, determined by its visibility and profile.

- The *security level of the system.*

4.5 Attack Trees

Attack trees offer another approach to characterizing and analyzing threats. An attack tree is a logical diagram similar to a fault tree. An attack tree, or its cousin the attack graph, can be used as a source of metrics or as a stand-alone attack model. In this report, we cite it primarily as a source of threat metrics.

When building an attack tree, as illustrated in Figure 1, an analyst begins by defining the attacker's overarching goal. This goal serves as the top node in the tree. Subordinate nodes detail (1) the logical relationships among the actions an adversary might undertake to achieve the goal and (2) the actions themselves. Each unique path through the tree represents an attack scenario.

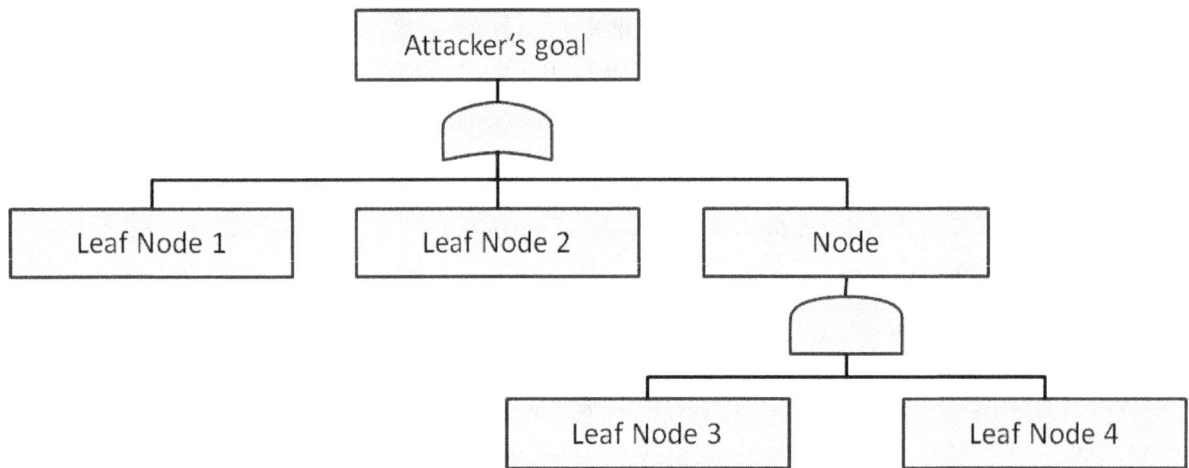

Figure 1: An example attack tree.

24

The example attack tree in Figure 1 shows an attack with three unique paths or scenarios. The attacker may pursue an attack comprising leaf node 1, leaf node 2, *or* a third attack that requires leaf node 3 *and* leaf node 4.

The threat analyst typically characterizes the attack scenarios using a variety of metrics. One metric, for example, might be the level of skill required to perform an attack. Another metric might be the time required to implement an attack. Still another might be the consequence generated by an attack. Once the analyst characterizes the scenarios using these metrics, she can rank the scenarios from the threat's perspective. Easy scenarios that yield an attractive consequence (again, from the threat's perspective) rise to the top. Difficult scenarios that yield weak or undesirable consequences sink to the bottom.

The threat analyst can apply the threat levels enumerated in the generic threat matrix directly to attack tree analysis. Once each attack path or scenario is defined (along with the metrics and measures for the leaf nodes) the analyst can assess which attacks each level of threat can perform.[8] For example, the analysis might yield the following tabulation (Table 4), which indicates that the ability to undertake the scenarios is distributed fairly evenly across the threat levels. (Note that the following tables and figures incorporate notional data.)

Table 4: Tabular view of attack tree scenarios by threat level (notional)

Threat Level	Scenarios	
	Number	Percent
1	9	90
2	8	80
3	8	80
4	8	80
5	8	80
6	7	70
7	6	60
8	3	30

Figure 2 displays the Table 4 data as a distribution. It should be clear that, taken as a whole, this set of attacks is not limited to high-level attackers.

Alternatively, the analysis might yield a result like that shown in Table 5 and Figure 3, which tell a very different story. In this case, the scenarios *are* limited to the higher-level attackers, with the exception of one scenario that an attacker of THREAT LEVEL 8 is able to perform. (This apparent anomaly can indeed occur, depending on the nature of the metrics applied.)

It is also possible to assess the output of the attack tree analysis metric-by-metric and compare this analysis with the threat levels. This assessment can tell the analyst which metrics are potentially the most interesting or influential and, additionally, which combinations of metric and threat level are also most interesting.

---

[8] The leaf nodes in the tree are the bottom-most or terminal nodes in each path. Leaf nodes are discrete actions. For each leaf node, the threat analyst estimates the values of the associated metrics.

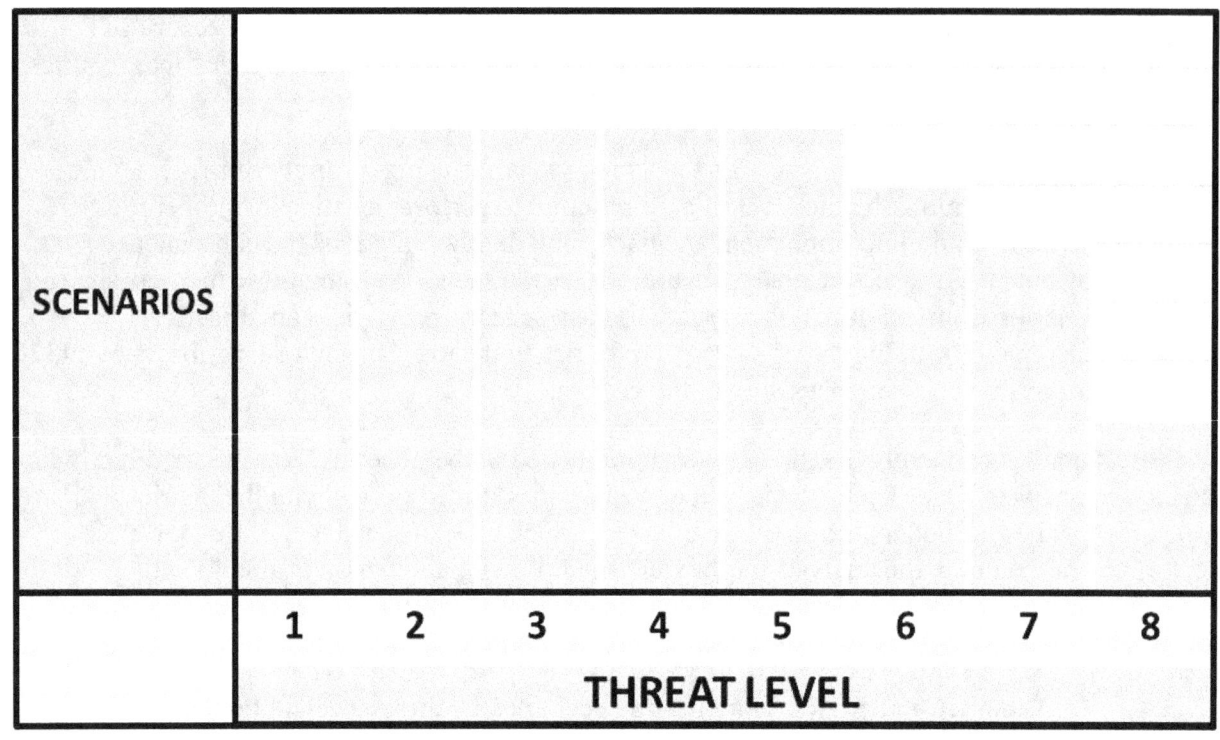

Figure 2: Chart view of attack tree scenarios by threat level (notional).

Table 5: Tabular view of alternative attack tree scenarios by threat level (notional)

Threat Level	Scenarios	
	Number	Percent
1	5	50
2	5	50
3	4	40
4	3	30
5	0	0
6	0	0
7	0	0
8	1	10

In sum, attack trees are useful in several ways. First, they allow the analyst to delineate attacks deductively. Second, they facilitate attack analysis by providing a transparent and relatively straightforward method of characterizing both attacks and attackers. Third, they are highly flexible and can be used to model just about any type of attack or threat. Finally, they generate data that can be used in concert with the generic threat model to learn more about which threats can undertake which attacks and which attacks are likely to be preferred by which threats. That said, attack trees represent only one way of thinking about attacks and threats. Not everyone prefers to approach the problem deductively, and some users no doubt find the logical structure of the tree to be more of a hindrance than a help.

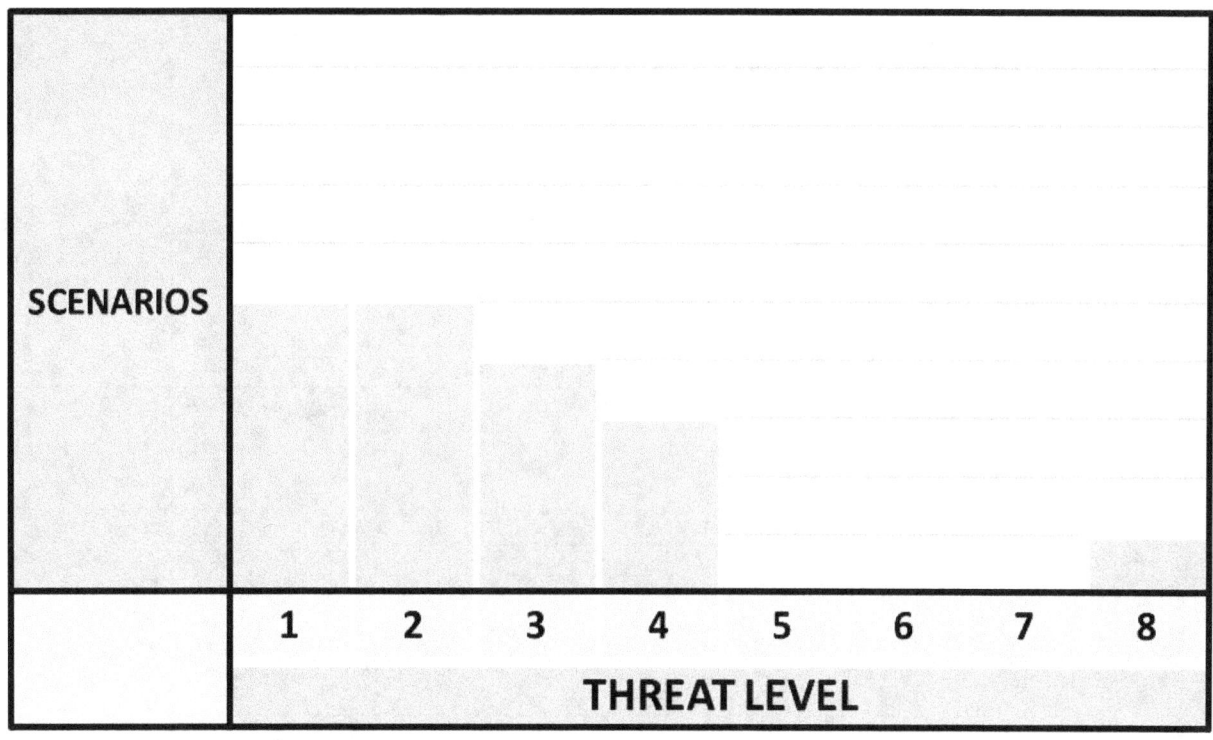

Figure 3: Chart view of alternative attack tree scenarios by threat level (notional).

4.6 Attack Frequency

Attack frequency can serve as another useful metric. It is particularly valuable because it can be coupled with a variety of related metrics. Attack frequency by level of difficulty is a potentially useful combination. Other possible combinations are attack frequency by target type and difficulty and attack frequency by vulnerability. Figure 4 illustrates a family of four charts that show the cumulative attack frequency by threat level and vulnerability for a given target type. The data are strictly notional.

We can just as easily generate a series of charts for cumulative attack frequency by target type for a given vulnerability (see Figure 5). Again, the data are strictly notional.

These kinds of charts complement the generic threat matrix and apply existing metrics in new and informative ways.

4.7 Making Security Measurable™

The MITRE Corporation is currently leading an effort to improve "the measurability of security through enumerating baseline security data, providing standardized languages as means for accurately communicating the information, and encouraging the sharing of the information with users by developing repositories" [9]. Initiatives within this effort include those listed in Table 6. Additional enumerations, languages, and repositories are identified on the MITRE Web site.

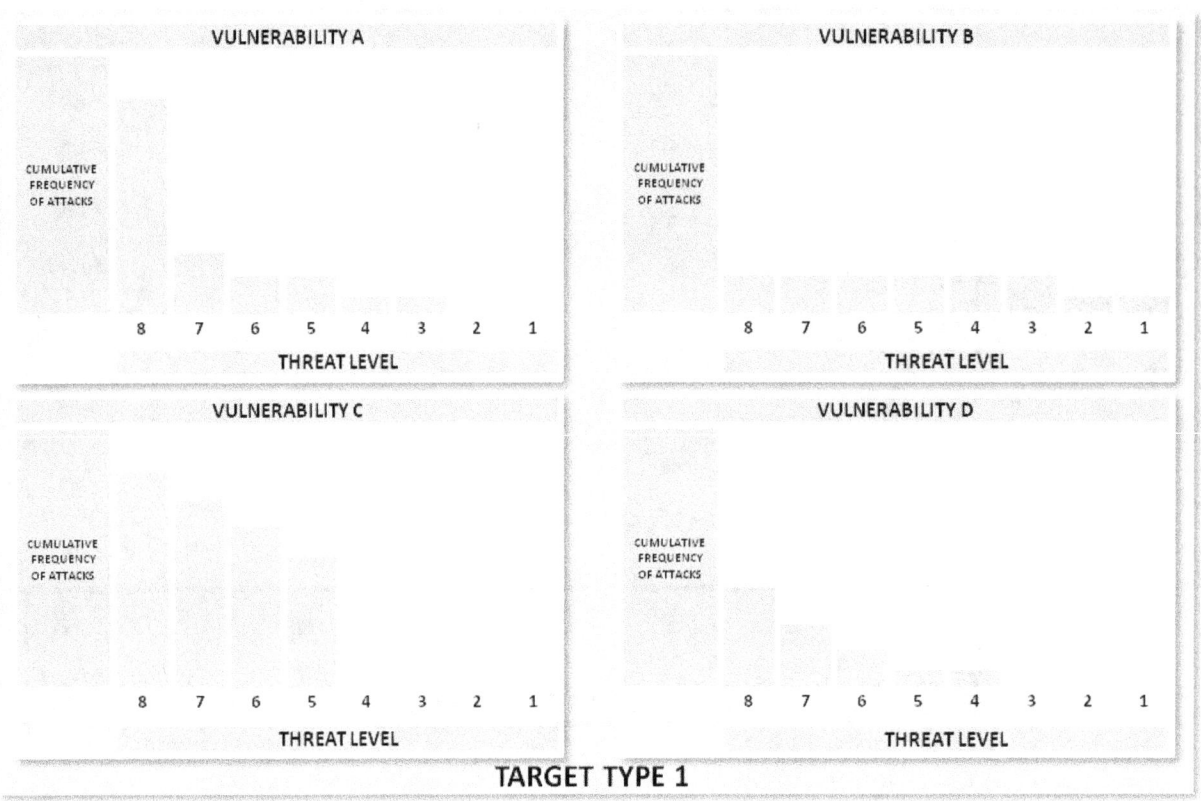

Figure 4: Cumulative attack frequency by threat level, vulnerability, and target type (notional).

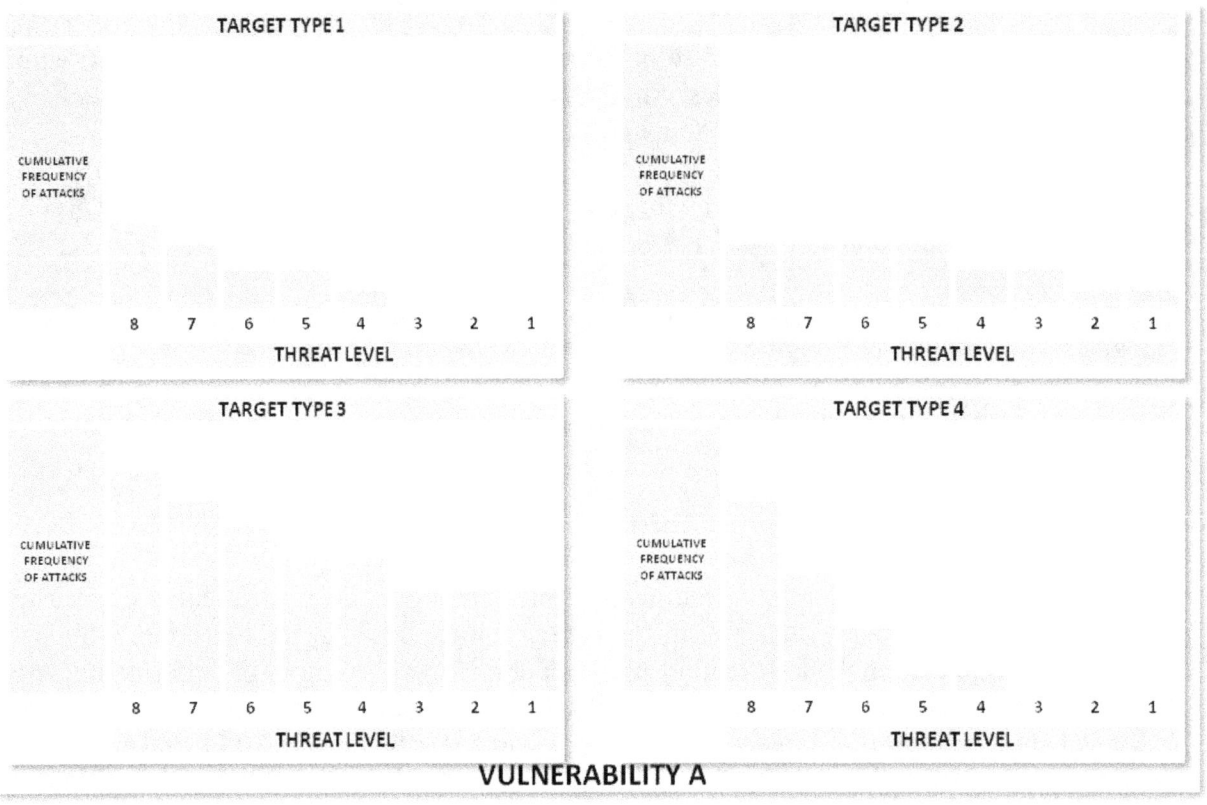

**Figure 5: Cumulative attack frequency by threat level, target type, and vulnerability (notional). **

28

Table 6: Selected enumerations, languages, and repositories in MITRE's Making Security Measurable initiative

Enumerations	Common Vulnerabilities and Exposures (CVE®)
	Common Weakness Enumeration (CWE™)
	Common Attack Pattern Enumeration and Classification (CAPEC™)
	Common Configuration Enumeration (CCE™)
Languages	Open Vulnerability and Assessment Language (OVAL®)
	Common Event Expression (CEE™)
	Malware Attribute Enumeration and Characterization (MAEC™)
Repositories	OVAL Repository

At a high level, the effort appears to be designed to standardize the categorization and description of security-related incidents, threats, and vulnerabilities so these things can then be counted and analyzed. This is accomplished by using what are, in effect, nominal or categorical scales. Thus, if one set of enumerations identifies 10 classes of "things," the analyst can then count how many of each "thing" occurs over a period of time. The descriptions are standardized using languages that yield "tool-consumable" data. This also facilitates automation. Finally, the "tool-consumable" data are held in shared repositories [10].

This initiative is potentially useful, and it becomes even more useful as more organizations join the effort. It is worth noting, however, that nominal scales tend to be more limited than ordinal, interval, and ratio scales or measurement. They are generally easier to define and easier to employ, but the resulting data cannot be (or should not be) used in as many quantitative operations.

This page intentionally blank

5 CONCLUSION: TOWARD A CONSISTENT THREAT ASSESSMENT PROCESS

To this point in our effort, we have used the generic threat matrix as our primary threat model. As such, the matrix serves as the framework for ordering a set of relevant threat metrics. These metrics vary in character from potentially quite subjective (the level of intensity) to relatively objective (the number of technical personnel). This is not surprising: Threat metrics can be difficult to identify, delimit, and quantify. In Section 4, we introduced a number of sources for additional threat metrics. Some of these metrics complement the generic threat matrix and others extend it.[9]

Regardless of the model or metrics employed, however, we recognize that we must also apply a consistent threat analysis *process*. Consistency is a key requirement of this effort (as noted in Section 0).

Figure 6 offers a functional view of the process employed to date. (We refer to this process as the "as is" process—as opposed to the suggested "to be" process, which we introduce later in this section.) Although the boxes and lines suggest a rigid process, the process in practice is anything but rigid. Indeed, the analysis of threat remains grounded in each analyst's experience, background, and expert opinion.

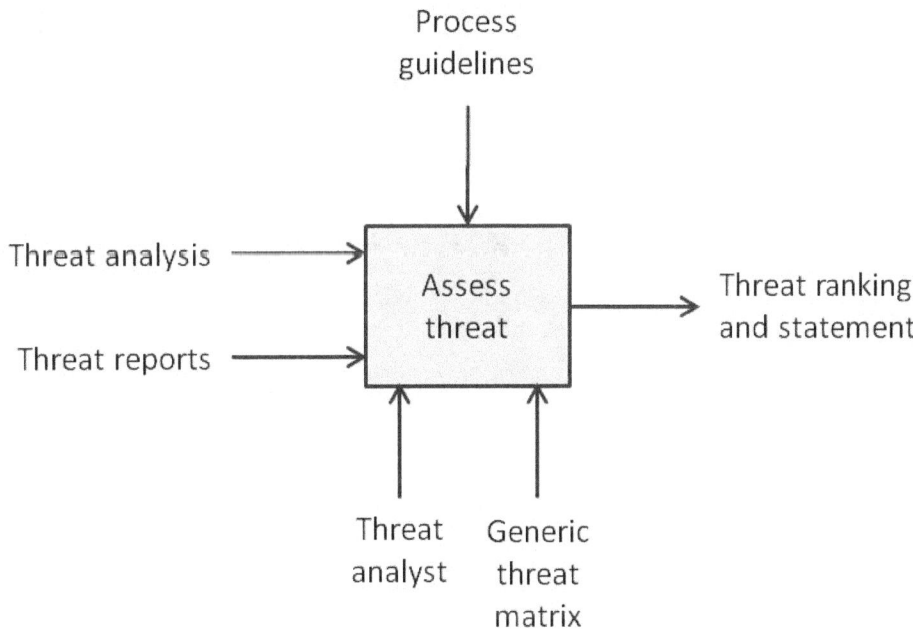

Figure 6: A functional view of the "as is" threat assessment process.

Figure 6: A functional view of the "as is" threat assessment processFigure 6 is a simple functional diagram where the main function (*assess threat*) is fed by two inputs (*threat analysis*

---

[9] Of course, the generic threat matrix is not the only possible threat model. Attack trees, for example, represent both a possible alternative *and* complement to the generic threat matrix (see Section 4.5).

and *threat reports*) and yields a single output (a *threat ranking and statement*). *Process guidelines* serve as a control, and the *threat analyst* and the *generic threat matrix* serve as resources.

What does the "as is" process lack? The main deficit is any explicit accommodation for feedback and learning. If we assume that the threat analyst generates useful threat rankings and statements, we should also assume that these outputs can serve as useful inputs in future iterations. In other words, the more we learn, the more we should feed what we have learned back through the process.

Figure 7 illustrates one possible variation. Here, three inputs inform the threat assessment: (1) relevant threats, (2) new threat information, and (3) catalogued threat information. The output, a threat report, becomes an input to future threat assessments.

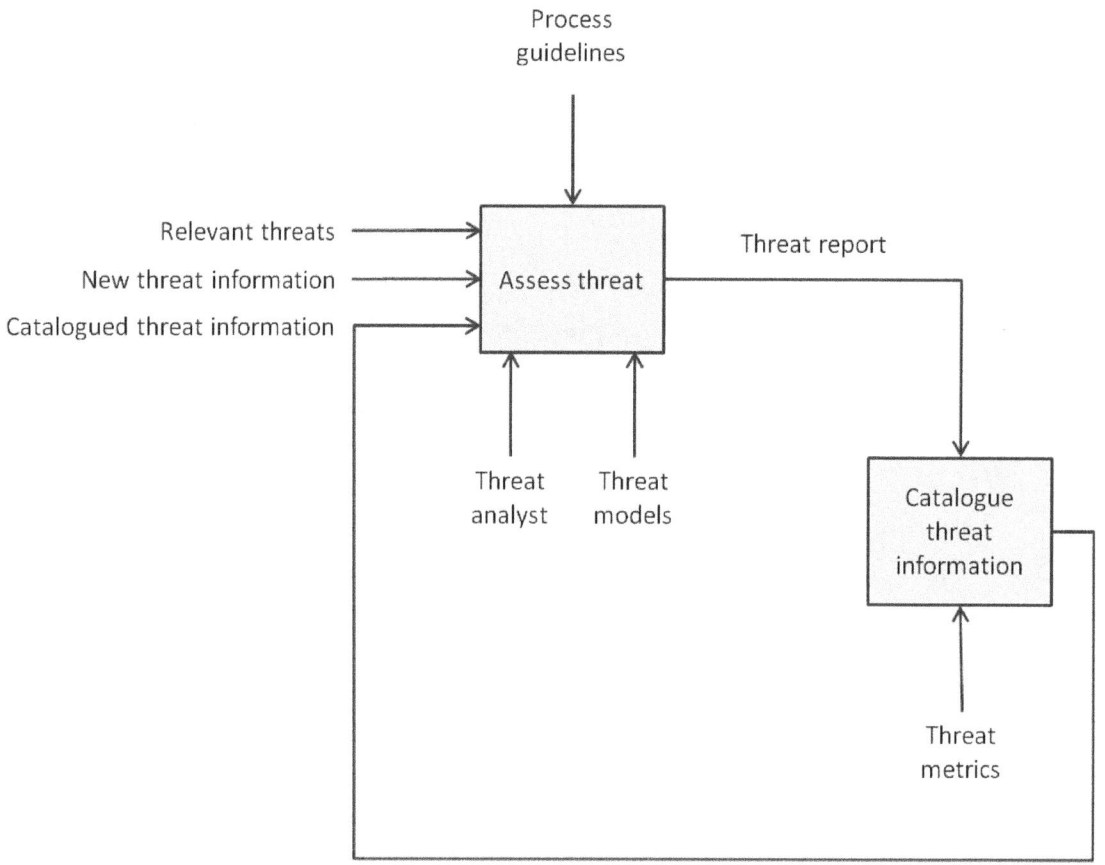

Figure 7: A functional view of the "to be" threat assessment process

Basically, routine and ongoing FCEB threat assessment research would discover and track threats (including general, unattributed threat activity), recording information in a database using the metrics defined here. For each agency that the RVA program is assessing, a search is conducted to identify threats relevant to that agency, possibly adding new information as it is discovered. Then the threat characteristic contained in the database is provided to the

32

Vulnerability Assessment Program (VAP) team as the estimate for that system. This will help in providing consistent estimates to multiple agencies.

Despite our progress in this area, further study regarding how analysts assess threats is needed. We propose a study involving human subjects that do not have a deep background in cyber threat analysis in order to observe their methodology for investigating threat (using open data sources) and applying the proposed OTA measurement system. The purpose of the study would be to observe and explore the investigations and assessments made by novice threat analysts in their process of categorizing threat in a cyber environment. Future studies would be necessary to compare this novice approach to that of subject matter experts, such as experienced intelligence analysts.

This page intentionally blank

6 WORKS CITED

[1] Bodeau, Deb, Jenn Fabius-Greene, and Rich Graubart. *How Do You Assess Your Organization's Cyber Threat Level?* The MITRE Corporation, n.d.

[2] RVA Program (Sandia National Laboratories). *Operational Threat Assessment Project Execution Plan for a Single Threat Assessment (DRAFT).* Federal Network Security, Compliance & Assurance Program, U.S. Department of Homeland Security, 2010.

[3] Merriam-Webster.com. *metric.* http://www.merriam-webster.com/dictionary/metric (accessed September 15, 2011).

[4] Jaquith, Andrew. *Security Metrics: Replacing Fear, Uncertainty, and Doubt.* Upper Saddle River, NJ: Addison-Wesley, 2007.

[5] Frost, Bob. *Measuring Performance.* Dallas, TX: Measurement International, 2000.

[6] Kaydos, Will. *Operational Performance Measurement: Increasing Total Productivity.* Boca Raton, FL: St. Lucie Press, 1999.

[7] Frost, Bob. *Designing Metrics.* Dallas, TX: Measurement International, 2007.

[8] Duggan, D. P., S. R. Thomas, C. K. K. Veitch, and L. Woodard. *Categorizing Threat: Building and Using a Generic Threat Matrix.* Albuquerque, NM: Sandia National Laboratories, 2007.

[9] Martin, Robert A. *Making Security Measurable.* Bedford, MA: The MITRE Corporation. http://measurablesecurity.mitre.org/ (accessed October 13, 2011).

[10] Martin, Robert A. "Making Security Measurable and Manageable." *CrossTalk: The Journal of Defense Software Engineering*, September/October 2009: 26-32.

[11] DHS Risk Steering Committee. *DHS Risk Lexicon.* Washington, DC: The Department of Homeland Security, 2010.

This page intentionally blank

DISTRIBUTION

Mr. Robert Karas, Department of Homeland Security, 245 Murray Ln SW, Bldg. 410, Washington, DC 20528

| 1 | MS0671 | J. Mark Harris | 0527 |
| 1 | MS0899 | RIM-Reports Management, | 9532 (electronic copy) |

www.ingramcontent.com/pod-product-compliance
Lightning Source LLC
Chambersburg PA
CBHW081539280526
45788CB00010B/3297